Scotland Wildlife

Written by Anne Glennie

RISING ★ STARS

The Cairngorms Park is in the Highlands of Scotland.

Cairngorms Park

Scotland

The park has hills, pine forests and lakes.

You can go on a bike ride or camp out in a tent!

A bike ride in the forest

Camping in the Cairngorms

The park has lots of wildlife. You can spy all kinds of animals, birds, plants, and insects!

red squirrel

wildcat

pine marten

otter

rabbit

dragonfly

butterflies

pike

pine tree

Pine martens

Pine martens have brown fur and long tails. They have fine, pale neck fur.

pale fur

long tail

Pine martens make high cries, like a cat.
They have up to five kits* at a time.

*A **kit** is a baby pine marten.

Pine martens come out at night to hunt for food.

Pine martens eat insects and little animals like rabbits and squirrels.

This pine marten is looking for food.

Wildcats

Wildcats have light brown fur. Look at the spots, bands, and stripes on the side of this wildcat's coat.

Wildcats look like pet cats, but can't be tamed. There are not a lot of them left in the wild.

When wildcat kittens are born, they are blind and have fuzz-like fur.
Wildcats eat rabbits and even ducks.

This wildcat kitten likes to hide inside a pile of twigs!

fuzz-like fur

Scottish pike

The pike lives in lakes and rivers. It is one of the biggest Scottish fish.

Pike can be up to 150 cm long!

Pike hide in the dark, then swim out to grab fish or frogs to eat!

Will you come and see the Cairngorms Park one day?

Talk about the book

Answer the questions:

1 Where is the Cairngorms Park?

2 What is a baby pine marten called?

3 What do wildcats eat?

4 Why do you think the pike hides before it catches its food?

5 Do you think it's important to protect animals that live in the wild? Why or why not?

6 Have you ever been to a park like this? Would you like to visit one?